שָׁלוֹם וּבְרָכָה

BLACK-LINE MASTERS

by
Roberta Osser Baum

Illustrations by
Deborah Zemke

ISBN: 0-87441-697-3

Dear Educator,

Welcome to the *Shalom Uvrachah Funbook*, where every page is filled with lively activities to enrich your students' classroom experience as they learn to read Hebrew using *Shalom Uvrachah—The New Hebrew Primer.*

The purpose of the *Funbook* is six-fold:

1. Review and reinforce the new letters, vowels, and heritage words in *Shalom Uvrachah*

2. Provide additional writing practice

3. Engage students who come early to class

4. Challenge students who finish their regular class work early

5. Provide opportunities for pair- and team-learning

6. Make your students smile!

Structure of the Funbook:

There are 54 activity sheets in the book—approximately two sheets for each of the 25 lessons in *Shalom Uvrachah*. If two new letters and/or vowels are taught in a lesson in *Shalom Uvrachah*, then the Funbook will usually have an activity sheet for each new letter and/or vowel. Look at the "New Letters" or "New Vowels" heading at the top of each page to see the new item that is being introduced.

How to Use the Funbook:

When your students learn a new letter or vowel, photocopy the appropriate *Funbook* page for them. After using the worksheet in class, consider sending it home. You will give parents an insight into their child's classroom activities and perhaps even help them learn a bit of Hebrew! You'll notice, too, a family-page web address at the bottom of each page. Parents who go to that site will find an *alef-bet* chart, a calendar showing the dates on which all the Jewish holidays fall, and the blessings (in Hebrew, English translation, and transliteration) to help them celebrate the holidays.

We are eager to hear your reactions to these materials. Please write or call to let us know what worked best for you and your students. Meanwhile, we hope your class has lots of fun!

B'hatslaḥah,

Terry Kaye
Director of Educational Services

Name _____

Button Up

Connect the dots to make a button inside the letter Bet.

Put a dot in each letter to make a Bet.

Write Bet here. _____

Circle each Bet.

בּ בּ בּ תּ בּ תּ בּ תּ בּ תּ

How many times did you circle Bet? _____

Tav Times Two

What is the name of this letter? תּ _____

What is the name of this letter? ת _____

Write the two letters here. _____ _____

Circle each Tav.

תּ תּ בּ תּ תּ תּ בּ תּ תּ בּ תּ

How many times did you circle Tav? _____

The word בַּת means "daughter." Write it here. _____

What is the name of the first letter in the word בַּת? _____

Name _____

Up, Up, and Away

These four balloons
are floating
in the air.

Write each balloon's
letter on the lines in
the balloon to bring
it down to earth.

Then write the *name*
of the letter on the
string.

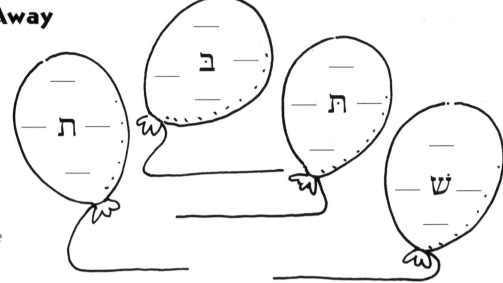

Open the Lock

You and a classmate
can open each lock
by reading the
word-parts and
words to each other.

Name _____

Word Find

Read all the sounds on each game board to a classmate. Find and circle the word שַׁבָּת on each game board. Look across, up and down, and diagonally.

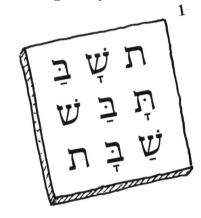

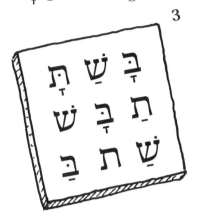

Light It!

Write each letter on the flame of the matching candle.

Write שַׁבָּת.

_____

ב שׁ ת

Tav　　　Bet　　　Shin

Matching Game

Draw lines to connect the sound-alikes in each column.

Write the three sets of matching sounds on the lines below.

_____ _____ _____

שִׁ	בִּ
תָּ שַׁ	שׁ
בֶּ	תַּ

Name _____

Circle Time

Circle each Mem on the matzah.

How many times did you circle Mem? _____

Write Mem the same number of times.

_____

Checkout Line

Put a ✓ on the line if all the sounds are the same.
Put an ✗ on the line if the sounds are different.

שָׁ שַׁ שָׁ שָׁ _____ .1

מָ מַ מֶ מָ _____ .2

בּ ת מ ת _____ .3

מָ בַּ שָׁ תַּ מָ בַּ _____ .4

ת תָ תַ תָ _____ .5

Write the word-part that is...

a sound a sheep makes _____   another name for "mommy" _____

a way to say "be quiet" _____

Bowl-a-Thon

Write the Hebrew letter that matches the English sound on each bowling pin.

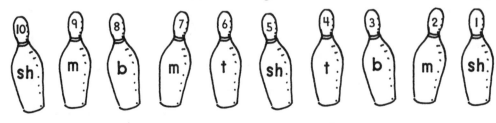

____ ____ ____ ____ ____ ____ ____ ____ ____ ____

Name _____

Candy Clues

Can you and a classmate read the sound on each candy?

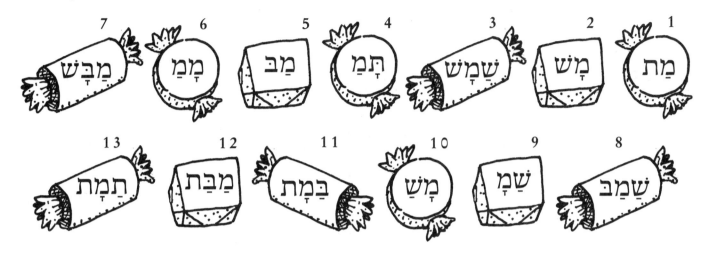

Ḥanukkah Lights

Write the word שַׁמָשׁ above the helper candle.

Then write the correct Hebrew letter above each of the other eight candles.

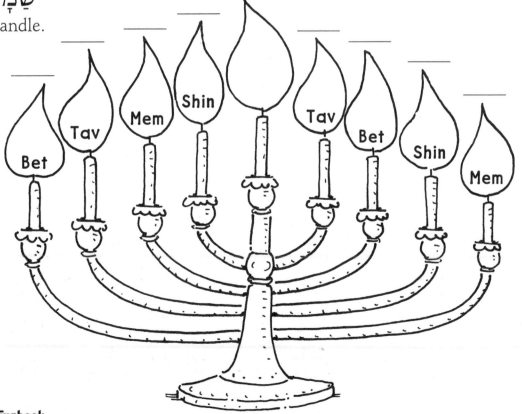

Name _____

Colors of the Rainbow

Use the same color crayon or marker to color
the two letters on each rainbow that are the same.

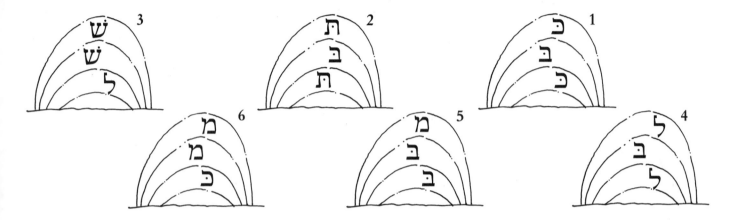

Name Game

Connect the Hebrew
letter to its name.

What sound does the
letter make?

Circle the sound in
its name.

Kaf 1 — שׁ	Lamed 2 — ל	Kaf 1 — שׁ

Bet
Mem   כּ   3
Kaf

Lamed
Tav   ל   2
Kaf

Kaf
Shin   שׁ   1
Lamed

Tav
Mem   ת   6
Lamed

Kaf
Tav   בּ   5
Bet

Lamed
Mem   מ   4
Shin

Relay Race

Partner #1 reads the first word-part.
Partner #2 reads the first and second word-parts.
Partner #3 reads all three word-parts. Then switch roles.

4. שַׁמַ תָּת כַּלָשׁ   1. כָּל בַּמָ לָל

5. בָּשַׁ תָּכ לָמַת   2. מָשׁ כַּבָ תַלַת

6. לָלָכ כַּמָשׁ כַּלָת   3. שַׁבָּת כָּלָב מַכָשׁ

Name _____

Step by Step

Connect the dots to complete each footprint. Read each word as you "walk."

4 שֶׁמֶשׁ 3 שַׁבָּת 2 בַּת 1 כַּלָּה

8 בָּלַת 7 לָמָה 6 הַכַּלָּה 5 כַּלַּת

Who Am I?

Fill in the blanks with the correct word.

בַּת   כַּלָּה   שֶׁמֶשׁ   שַׁבָּת

• I begin on Friday evening and end on Saturday night. _____

• Just as Shabbat is welcomed, so too am I joyously welcomed

  at a wedding ceremony. _____

• I am used to light the eight candles on the *ḥanukkiah*. _____

• I am the girl in my home. _____

Tic-Tac-Toe

Play tic-tac-toe with a friend.

Read the sounds correctly to make an X or an O.

3

מָמָ	בָּה	בַּת
בְּכָ	הַל	כָּלַ
הַשׁ	תֵה	שָׁכֵ

2

מֵ	לָ	בָּ
הֵ	כֵּ	שׁ
מ	שֵׁ	כָּ

1

ל	בָּ	כֵּ
תָ	הֵ	שָׁ
כ	לָ	מַ

New Vowel : **New Letter** ר

Name _____

Circle Time

Read each line.

Circle the two letters on each line that are the same.

What sound do they make? Write the sound on the blanks.

____	ר	שׁ	מ	ל	כּ	ר	ת	.1
____	ה	שׁ	ר	כּ	ת	מ	כּ	.2
____	ר	ת	ל	כּ	שׁ	ת	בּ	.3
____	ה	ל	בּ	מ	ר	בּ	כּ	.4
____	מ	שׁ	ת	ה	ל	ר	.5

Twins

Read the sounds on each line.

Two sounds on each line are the same. Draw a box around each of them.

תָּ	לַ	רַ	כְּ	רָ	.1
בְ	מְ	תִּ	תַּ	מְ	.2
כִּ	שַׁ	הַ	שָׁ	רַ	.3
הַ	רְ	לְ	תָּ	הַ	.4
מָ	כְּ	הִ	כִּ	לַ	.5

New Vowel	New Letters
ְ	ר כ

Name ______________________________

Bingo

Write the Hebrew letters in the correct spaces on the card to win at Bingo.

ר ת בּ ה כ

תּ ל מ כּ שׁ

Lamed	Resh	Hay	Kaf
Chaf	Bet	Tav	Resh
Mem	Shin	Lamed	Bet
Kaf	Chaf	Shin	Tav

Fruit of the Tree

Read the Hebrew word on each apple. Then write the English meaning on the line above the apple.

Do you know the בְּרָכָה that we recite before we eat the fruit of the tree?

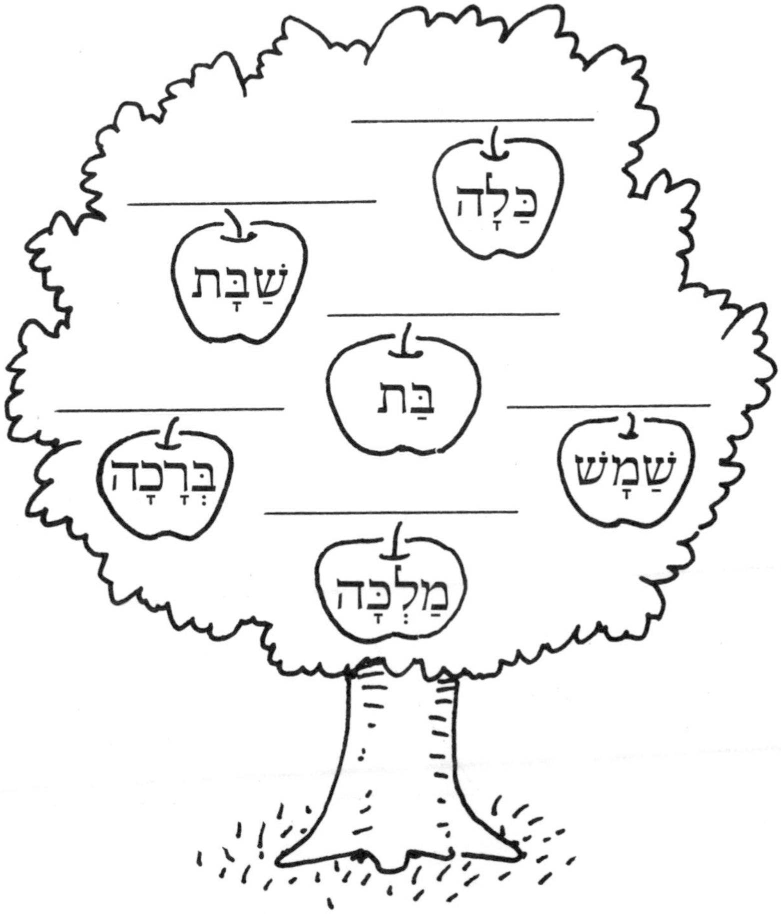

New Vowel	New Letter
־ְ	בּ

Name _____

Reach the Top

Climb the ladder by saying the name
and the sound of the letter on each rung.

Then circle the letter on the rung that matches
the letter at the top of the ladder.

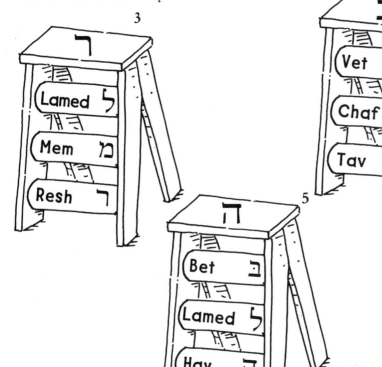

Pyramid Partners

Read the words on the pyramid
to a classmate. Then have your
classmate read the words back
to you.

Write the word on the
pyramid that means
"blessing."

Name _____

Green Thumb

Color the leaf with the Hebrew letter that matches the name in the flower.

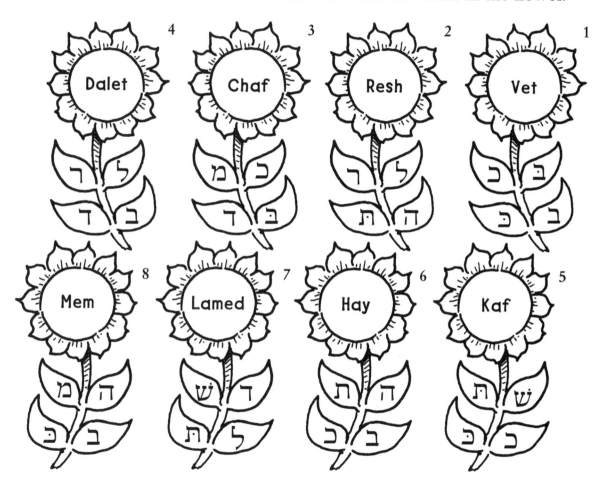

Star of David

Color each shape containing a ד
to see the Star of David.

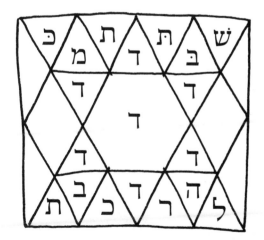

New Letter
א

Name _____

Silent Partner

Cross out the letter in each pair that makes no sound.
Write the sound of the other letter.

ב א ___   ש א ___   ר א ___   ב א ___

א ד ___   ל א ___   כ א ___   א מ ___

The Sounds of Music

Three sounds in each musical note rhyme. Put a ✓ next to the rhyming sounds in each musical note.

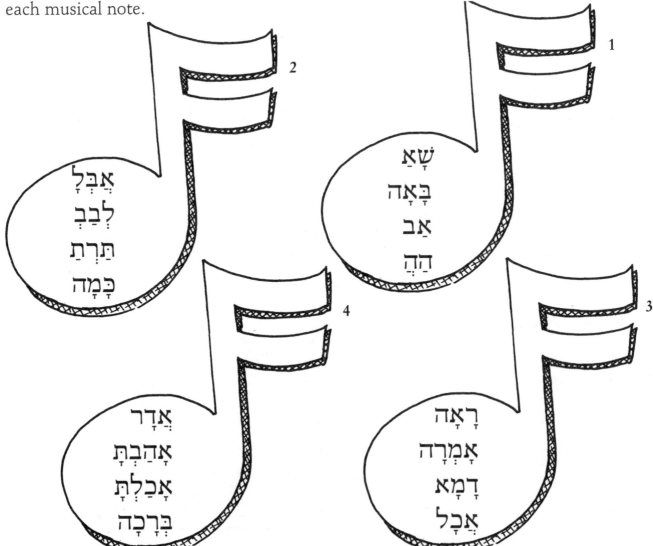

New Letters
א ו

Name _____

Same Sound

Write the letter ב. _____   Write the letter ת. _____

Write the letter ו. _____   Write the letter ת. _____

What sound do they both make? _____   What sound do they both make? _____

Read each word below.

Draw a circle around each א. Draw a box around each ה that makes no sound.

אָכְלָה   הַבְדָלָה   אֲבָדָה   בְּרָכָה   אַהֲבָה   הָוָה

When is the letter ה quiet like the letter א? _____

Sukkot Harvest

Complete the harvest by writing
each Hebrew word below in a basket.

דָבָר   דְבַשׁ

וְאָכַל   וְאָהַבְתָּ

וְכָל   אַתָּה

הַבְדָלָה   אַהֲבָה

Name _____

Same Sound

Write the sound-alike letters on the correct lines.

כ ת ו ק ב ת

_____ _____ _____
T   V   K

Circle the sound-alike letters on each line below.
Write their sound.

_____	ק	א	כ	ב	מ	ב	1.
_____	שׁ	ר	ב	ת	ו	א	2.
_____	כ	ת	ד	ו	ה	ת	3.
_____	ק	כ	ב	כ	ל	ו	4.
_____	ד	ת	ר	ו	ב	ה	5.

What's Missing?

① Add the missing letter ק to complete each word.
Write the meaning of each word.

_____ בָּלַת שַׁבָּת ___

_____ צְדָ__ה

③ Add the missing letter שׁ to
complete each word.
Write the meaning of each word.

_____ בָּת __

_____ מָשׁ __

② Add the missing letter כ to complete each word.
Write the meaning of each word.

_____ לָה __

_____ מַלְ__ה

Name _____

Gone Fishing

Write the letter in its matching fish.

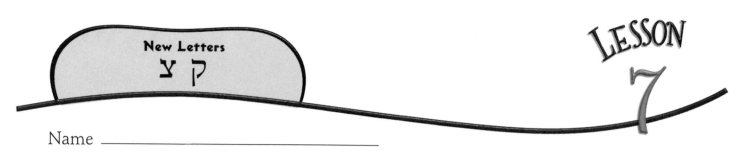

ד ה ה מ צ ו ק ת ר א כ

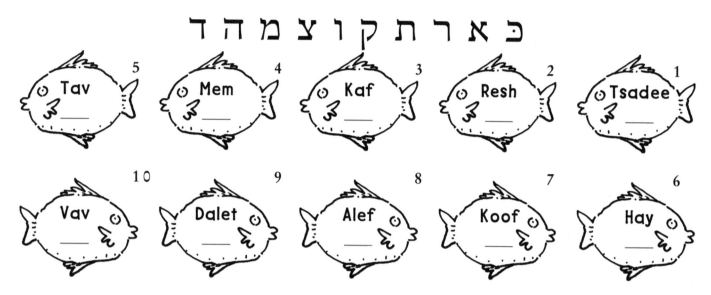

Relay Race

Partner #1 reads the first word-part.

Partner #2 reads the second word-part.

Partner #3 reads the whole word. Then switch roles.

2. צְדָ קָה צְדָקָה   1. מַ צָה מַצָה

4. קָ צָר קָצָר   3. אֲדָ מָה אֲדָמָה

6. קָ צָת קְצָת   5. צַ וָאר צַוָאר

Picture Perfect

Draw a line to connect each picture with its matching Hebrew word.

שַׁבָּת
מַצָה
צְדָקָה

בְּרָכָה
צְדָקָה
כַּלָה

שֶׁמֶשׁ
וְאָהַבְתָּ
כַּלָה

בְּבַקָשָׁה
הַבְדָלָה
קַבָּלַת

מַצָה
אַתָּה
אַהֲבָה

Name _____

Ring Toss

Choose the correct letter to write inside each ring.

High Score: 16 points.

א ש ב ו ת כ ר ל
ת ב ק ד ה צ מ כ

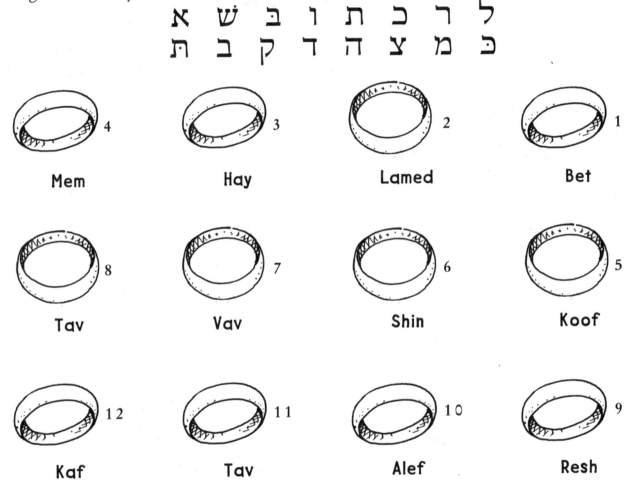

4 Mem	3 Hay	2 Lamed	1 Bet
8 Tav	7 Vav	6 Shin	5 Koof
12 Kaf	11 Tav	10 Alef	9 Resh
16 Chaf	15 Dalet	14 Tsadee	13 Vet

Now write the vowel ָ or ַ below each letter and practice reading each sound.

Name _____

Hebrew Riddles

Read the sounds below. Choose the sound that answers the riddle and write it on the line.

שִׁי מִי

I am myself. _____

תִּי הַ

You drink me from a cup. _____

בְּ קַ

I open a door. _____

בִּי לַ

I make sweet honey. _____

שִׁי הַ

I am a girl. _____

הִי שִׁי

I am a boy. _____

Computer Wiz

Read each letter name and write the Hebrew letter on the computer keyboard.

1. Bet
2. Tsadee
3. Mem
4. Resh
5. Koof
6. Alef
7. Tav
8. Lamed
9. Kaf
10. Vet
11. Shin
12. Tav
13. Hay
14. Chaf
15. Vav
16. Dalet

Name _____

What's Missing?

Fill in the blank to complete the pattern in each row.

<u>Pattern #1</u>

1 . _____ לְ קִי מְ לָ קִי

2 . _____ הִי אֶ צִי הִי אֶ

3 . _____ בְּלִי הִיא אִמָּא בְּלִי הִיא

4 . _____ צַדִּיק דָּוִד צִיצִית צַדִּיק דָּוִד

5 . _____ בִּימָה בַּר תִּיק בִּימָה בַּר

Can you recognize a boy's name in the lines above? Write it here. _____

What is the Hebrew word for "fringes on the corner of a tallit"? _____

<u>Pattern #2</u>

6 . קַדִּיש מִצְוָה אִשָּׁה קַדִּיש _____ אִשָּׁה

7 . רַבִּי הַתִּקְוָה אָבִיב רַבִּי _____ אָבִיב

8 . הִיא בְּרִית שְׁמִי הִיא _____ שְׁמִי

9 . דָּתִי קָצִיר מִילָה דָּתִי _____ מִילָה

10 . שִׁירָה צִוָּה אֲוִיר שִׁירָה _____ אֲוִיר

Can you recognize the name of the Israeli national anthem in the lines above?
Write it here. _____

Find the Hebrew word for "commandment." Write it here. _____

Name _____

Drumbeat

Draw a pair of drumsticks on each drum whose letter makes a sound.

How many pairs of drumsticks did you draw? _____

What sound does the letter make? _____

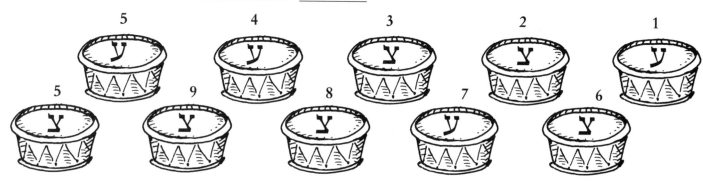

Checkout Line

Put a ✓ on the line if the pairs of sounds are the same.
Put an ✗ on the line if the pairs of sounds are different.

1.___ עִ עֲ   2.___ עֲ צֳ   3.___ עֲ אִ   4.___ בְּ תַ   5.___ כִּי קֳ

6.___ וְ רְָ   7.___ וּ בְּ   8.___ צֳ אֲָ   9.___ רְ דִי   10.___ אֲָ עֲ

Tongue Twisters

Can you read each line to your partner without twisting your tongue?

1. עָ   עֲ   עַ   עָ   עִי   עֲ   עְ

2. עֲ   עְ   עָ   צִי   עְ   עַ   עְ

3. עֲ   עַ   עְ   צִי   עְ   עֲ   עָ

4. עְ   עֲ   עָ   צִי   עֲ   עְ   עְ

Name _____

Tic-Tac-Toe

Play tic-tac-toe with a friend. Read the sounds correctly to make an X or an O.

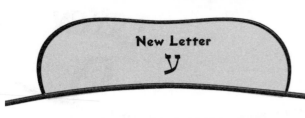

High Five

Draw a ring on the finger that matches the letter name on the palm of the hand. Then, give your partner a "high five" by naming all five letters on each hand and their sounds.

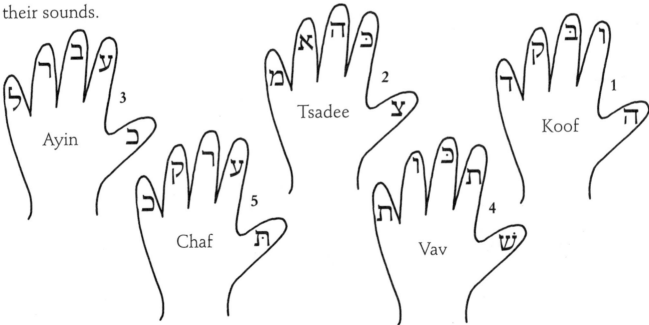

Name _____

Writing עִבְרִית

עִבְרִית means "Hebrew."

Practice writing each word בְּעִבְרִית—in Hebrew—on the line next to the word.

4. שְׁמַע _____   1. עִבְרִית _____

5. עֲמִידָה _____   2. צִיצִית _____

6. אַרְבַּע _____   3. מַעֲרִיב _____

Relay Race

Partner #1 reads the first word-part.
Partner #2 reads the second word-part.
Partner #3 reads the whole word. Then switch roles.

1. שְׁמַע   מַע   שְׁ   4. שָׁעָה   עָה   שָׁ

2. עֲמִידָה   דָה   עֲמִי   5. עָתִיד   תִיד   עָ

3. דַעַת   עַת   דַ   6. עֲתִיקָה   קָה   עֲתִי

Which words above are the names of prayers? Write them below.

_____   _____

New Letters
נ ן

Name _____

Bingo for One

Write the number of the letter name in its matching box.
Fill your entire Bingo card.

1. Lamed	5. Kaf	9. Alef	13. Vav
2. Ayin	6. Vet	10. Dalet	14. Shin
3. Hay	7. Resh	11. Tav	15. Mem
4. Nun	8. Tsadee	12. Final Nun	16. Chaf

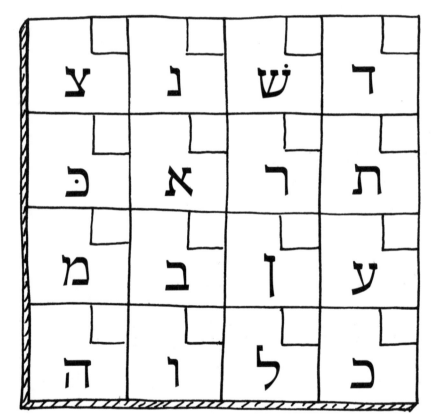

Bingo Bonus

What sound does each pair of letters make? Write the sound on the line.

4. כ ק   3. ת ת   2. ב ו   1. נ ן

_____   _____   _____   _____

Name _____

Knock, Knock

Open the doors by writing the meaning of the Hebrew words on the door.

| prophet | helper | separation | and you shall love | Shabbat |

| blessing | bride | hear | justice | commandment |

3 צְדָקָה _____

2 שַׁבָּת _____

1 נָבִיא _____

7 מִצְוָה _____

6 הַבְדָלָה _____

5 שֶׁמֶשׁ _____

4 כַּלָה _____

10 שְׁמַע _____

9 בְּרָכָה _____

8 וְאָהַבְתָּ _____

Name _____

Catching Practice

Draw a line to connect the glove and the ball that make the same sound.

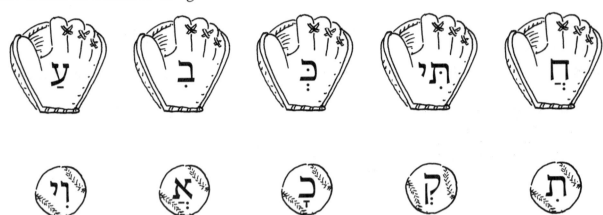

A Home Run

In each ballgame, read the sounds on each base correctly to a classmate to score a home run. Color the diamond when you score a home run.

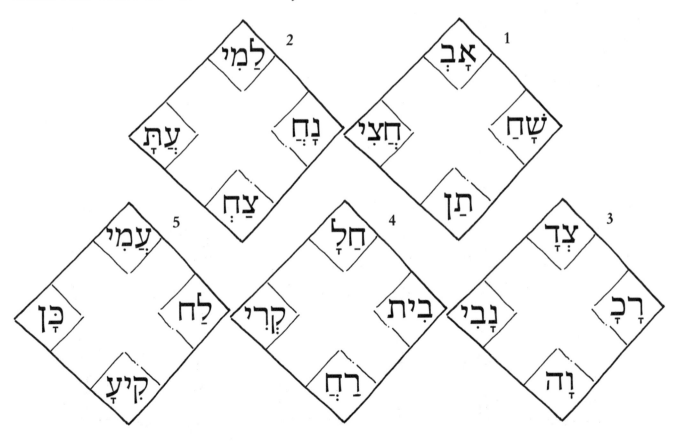

Name _____

Beachcombers

Draw a seashell around each word on the beach. Then, collect the shells by reading the word on each one to your beach buddy.

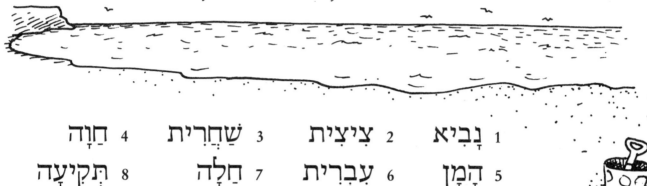

1 נָבִיא   2 צִיצִית   3 שַׁחֲרִית   4 חַוָּה

5 הָמָן   6 עִבְרִית   7 חַלָּה   8 תְּקִיעָה

Which Hebrew name is part of the Purim story? _____

Rain, Rain, Go Away

Choose a letter and a vowel. Write the letter-vowel combination inside a raindrop. Repeat until all ten raindrops are filled. Read your combinations to a classmate to make the rain stop!

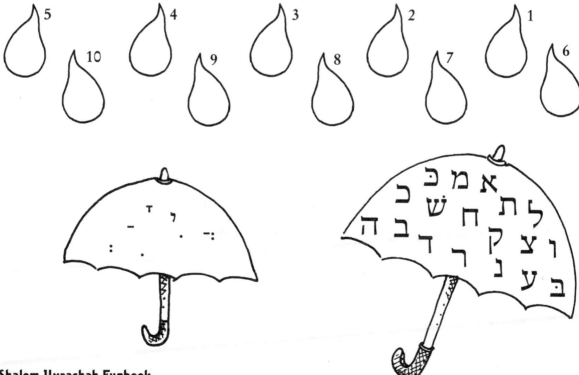

New Letter
ל

Name _____

Building Blocks

Read the letter name and circle the correct letter—ן, ו, י—in each building block.

ו ז י	ו ז י	ו י ז
Yud	**Vav**	**Final Nun**
ו ז י	ז י ו	ז י
Vav	**Final Nun**	**Yud**
ו ז י	ז י ו	ז י ו
Final Nun	**Yud**	**Vav**

ו ז י	ו ז י	ו ז י
Yud	**Vav**	**Final Nun**
ו ז י	ו ז י	ו ז י
Vav	**Final Nun**	**Yud**
ו ז י	ו ז י	ו ז י
Final Nun	**Yud**	**Vav**

Hand in Hand

Read the word on each hand to a classmate. Then listen to your classmate read.
Shake hands when you're done!

6 הַשְּׁבִיעִי 5 נָבִיא 4 יָד 3 עָלֶיהָ 2 מִנְיָן 1 יִצְחָק

12 צַדִּיק 11 בְּרִית 10 עַיִן 9 שִׁירָה 8 קָדִימָה 7 הַלַּיְלָה

Name _____

Lock and Key

Open the locks by reading the words to a classmate. Then challenge your classmate to read the words to you.

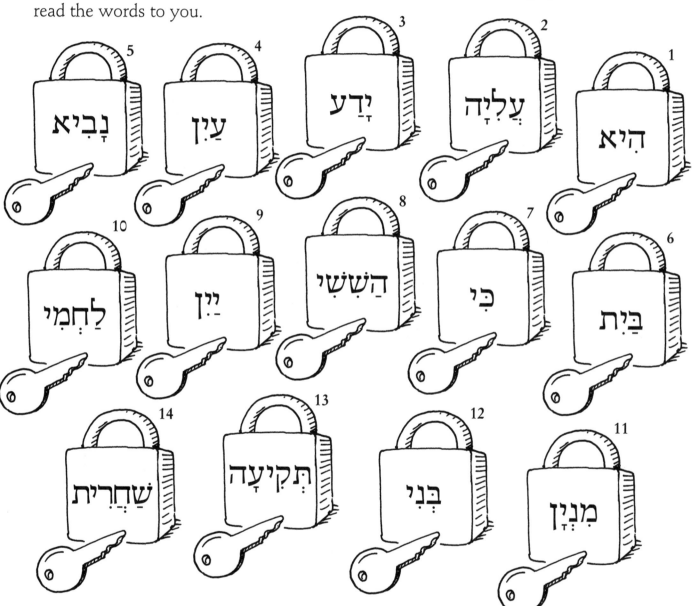

- Color the lock with the Hebrew word for "prophet."
- Put stripes in the lock with the Hebrew word for "going up."
- Put spots in the lock with the Hebrew word for "ten Jewish adults."
- Draw squiggly lines in the lock with the Hebrew word for a sound the shofar makes.

Name _____

Stop Signs

Color each stop sign that has a Final Mem. Then put stripes in each stop sign that has a Final Nun.

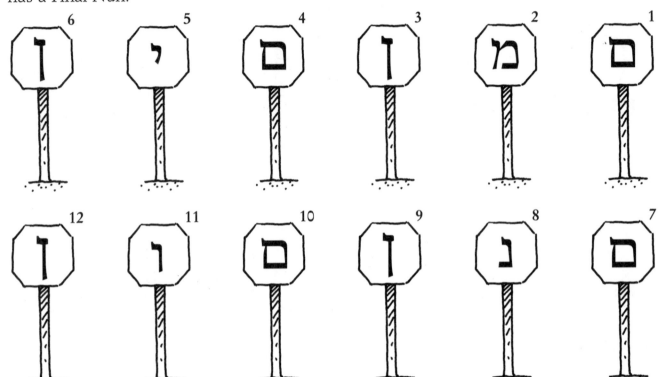

It's the End!

Add a Final Mem to each word below.

הָעֲמִי _   הַדְּבָרִי _   אַבְרָהָ _   אָדָ _ .1

מִַ _   הַמְּלָכִי _   חַיִּי _   יַלְדֵי _ .2

Add a Final Nun to each word below.

לְמַעַ _   בְּנְיָמִ _   נָתָ _   עִַ _ .1

מִשְׁכָּ _   מַאֲמִי _   וְרַחֲמָ _   מִנְיָ _ .2

Read the completed words to a reading partner.

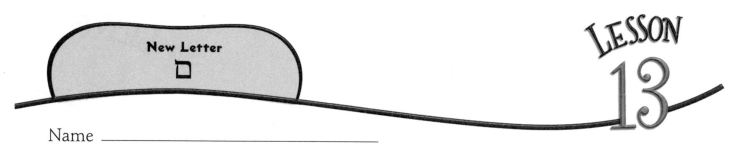
Name _____

Making Music

Write each letter on its matching musical note.

ל ת מ נ ב א כ ו צ י ק

ב ש ע ן ח ר ת כ ד מ ה

Can you point to and sing each letter name by making up your own melody for each one?

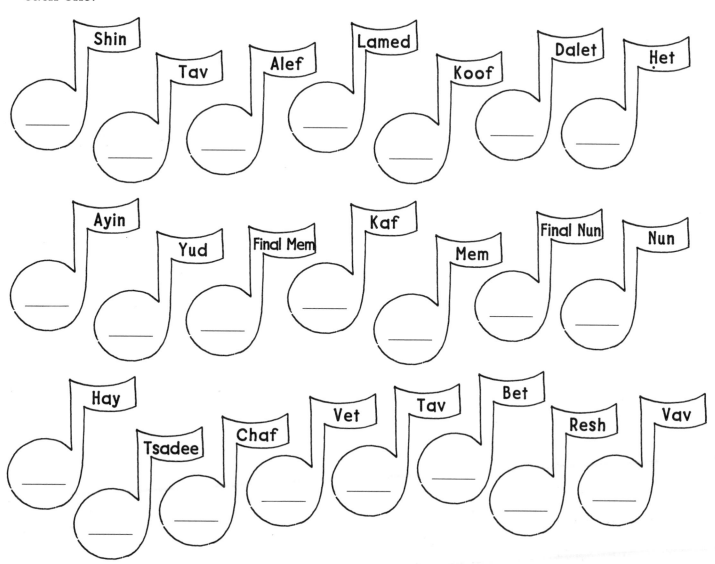

New Vowels

וֹ

Name _____

Stickball

Add a ball (dot) over each stick (Vav) to complete the vowel וֹ in the words below.
Then read the words.

1 . תּוֹרָה   קָדוֹשׁ   מוֹרָה   כְּבוֹד

2 . צִיוֹן   עוֹד   הוֹמִיָה   לִהְיוֹת

3 . עוֹלָם   תּוֹרָתוֹ   שָׁלוֹם   הַמוֹצִיא

Word Riddles

Complete the word that answers the question: *Who am I?*

Hint: You will find the answers in the "Stickball" game.

1 . I am read each week in the synagogue. I help us remember God's teachings.

Who am I?   תּוֹ_____

2 . I mean "peace."

Who am I?   שָׁ_____

3 . I am the name for the blessing over bread.

Who am I?   הַ_____

4 . I mean "holy."

Who am I?   קָ_____

5 . I am another word for "Israel."

Who am I?   צִ_____

6 . I am a teacher.

Who am I?   מוֹ_____

7 . I am the world.

Who am I?   עוֹ_____

Name _____

Same and Different

Circle the two letter-vowel sounds that are the *same* on each line.

1. כֶּ ק כְ קֶ ק כֹ
2. וּ בְ וֹ בֶּ וַ
3. כְ חֹ כ כֹ חֶ
4. עֹ אוֹ אָ עֹ אֹ

Circle the letter-vowel sound that is *different* on each line.

4. עֹ אוֹ אָ עֹ אֹ
5. תוּ תֶ תוֹ תֵ תֻ
6. כוּ תוֹ חוֹ ח

Colorful Balloons

Color each balloon lightly when you read its word correctly.

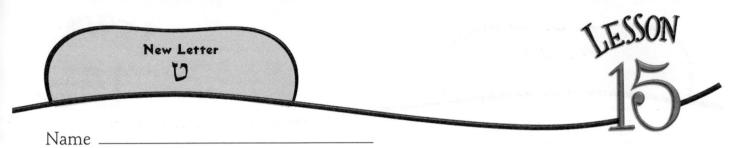
Name _____

Erev Shabbat

Write the sound-alike letters on the flames of each pair of candles.

ח ב א כ ו ט כ ע ת ק

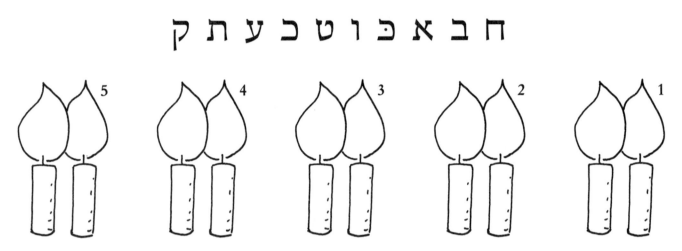

Say the sound each pair makes.

Word Find

Read all the sounds on each game board. Find and circle the word that appears above each game board. Look across, up and down, and diagonally.

שָׁלוֹם ³

שָׁ	אֲ	הוֹ
צֵ	לוֹ	שִׁי
ת	וּ	ם

תּוֹרָה ²

מוֹ	תּוֹ	חֵ
בְּ	רָ	כ
חַ	ה	טַ

טַלִּית ¹

טַ	ק	מֹ
לִי	עֲ	רְ
ת	שׁוֹ	בְּ

Write or draw the meaning of each word.

שָׁלוֹם _____

תּוֹרָה _____

טַלִּית _____

Name _____

Greeting Cards

Make "greeting cards" by writing one of the following phrases on each card below:

1. Name of the Jewish New Year — רֹאשׁ הַשָּׁנָה

2. New Year greeting — שָׁנָה טוֹבָה

3. Phrase meaning "holiday" or "festival" — יוֹם טוֹב

4. Wish for "a peaceful Shabbat" — שַׁבָּת שָׁלוֹם

5. Phrase meaning "bar mitzvah" — בַּר מִצְוָה

6. Phrase meaning "bat mitzvah" — בַּת מִצְוָה

Draw a matching picture on each card:

- shofar for רֹאשׁ הַשָּׁנָה
- apples and honey for שָׁנָה טוֹבָה
- Passover, Shavuot, or Sukkot picture for יוֹם טוֹב
- dove for שַׁבָּת שָׁלוֹם
- בַּר מִצְוָה for טַלִית
- בַּת מִצְוָה for בִּימָה

LESSON 16

Name _____

Eh, Eh, Eh

Read lines 1-4 to a reading partner.

Put a ✓ next to the line if you read it correctly.

1. ____ רֶ הֶ לֶ נֶ כֶּ מֶ טֶ שֶׁ וֶ חֶ

2. ____ תֶּם מֶן עֶה דֶּשׁ מֶת דֶּק לֶד

3. ____ לֶחֶם וָעֶד שֶׁמֶשׁ נֶאֱמַר מֹשֶׁה אֱמֶת

4. ____ קֹדֶשׁ הֹוֶה אֱלֹהִים שֶׁבַע עֶלְיוֹן יוֹשֶׁבֶת

Did You Know?

אֱלֹהִים is one way we say God's name in Hebrew.

Circle God's name—אֱלֹהִים—in the lines above.

Write אֱלֹהִים here. _____

Do you know another way to say God's name?

Word Link

Read the words to a reading partner. Draw a line from word to word as you read each one correctly.

←

אֲשֶׁר אָבוֹא אֱלֹהִים בְּרֹב אֶחָד שְׁלֹא

בֶּאֱמֶת קָדְשׁוֹ נֶאֱמָן נוֹדֶה לַצַדִּיק בּוֹאִי

New Vowels
ּ ָ

Name _____

Make Your Own Word Cards

Practice reading the heritage words below.

בְּרָכָה   צְדָקָה   אֱמֶת   עֲלִיָה   תּוֹרָה

מִצְוָה   שְׁמַע   שָׁלוֹם   קָדוֹשׁ   טַלִית

Then write one heritage word in each rectangle to create your own word cards.

3	2	1
_____	_____	_____

7	6	5	4
_____	_____	_____	_____

10	9	8
_____	_____	_____

Word Wiz

• Which word means "going up"? _____

• What does אֱמֶת mean? _____

• Write the word for "peace." _____

• Which word means "justice"? _____

New Letter
פ

Name _____

Penny in the Pocket

Put a dot in each letter to make a Pay.

פ פ פ פ פ פ פ פ פ פ

Circle each Pay.

ב פ ת פ כ פ פ ת פ ב כ

How many times did you circle Pay? _____

Draw a line to connect each letter to its name.

Pay	ב
Bet	כ
Tav	פ
Kaf	ת

Add the letter פ to complete each word.

כ_ָה   ע_ָרוֹן   מִשׁ_ָּחָה   _ֶּלֶא   _ִּתְאֹם   _ֶּרַח

Word Wiz

Draw a כִּפָּה.

List the members of your מִשְׁפָּחָה. _____

Relay Race

Partner #1 reads the first word.
Partner #2 reads the first and second words.
Partner #3 reads all three words. Then switch roles.

1. פֶּרֶק   עֶבֶד   פָּרָשָׁה   מֹשֶׁה   כָּמֹכָה   שָׁמַיִם

2. וַיֹּאמֶר   תְּקִיעָה   טוֹב   מִנְחָה   נְטִילַת   מִצְרַיִם

3. חַיִּים   אֱלֹהִים   אָרוֹן   שְׁמַע   מַצָּה   יַיִן

Name _____

Preparing for פֶּסַח

Put a ✓ next to the statements that are TRUE.
Put an ✗ next to the statements that are FALSE.

1. The English word for פֶּסַח is Passover. ____

2. We eat חַלָה at פֶּסַח. ____

3. We dip the שַׁמָשׁ in salt water at the פֶּסַח seder. ____

4. The book that tells the story of פֶּסַח is called the *haggadah*. ____

5. We may have a פֶּסַח seder with our כַּלָה. ____

6. God sent מֹשֶׁה to lead us from slavery to freedom. ____

7. The phrase שָׁנָה טוֹבָה is used at פֶּסַח. ____

8. We celebrate פֶּסַח in the month of נִיסָן. ____

In which statement would you substitute the word מַצָּה to make it TRUE? ____

Holiday Time

Write the פֶּסַח words in column 1. Write the other holiday words in column 2.

מֹשֶׁה   שָׁנָה טוֹבָה   מַצָּה   סְבִיבוֹן   רֹאשׁ הַשָׁנָה

אֲפִיקוֹמָן   יְצִיאַת מִצְרַיִם   הַגָדָה   הָמָן   תְּקִיעָה

2.   1.

_____   _____

_____   _____

_____   _____

_____   _____

Name _____

Pictionary Players

Create a "pictionary" in the following way:
Write the Hebrew for each English word.
Draw a picture to illustrate each word in your pictionary.

סְבִיבוֹן נָבִיא כִּפָּה צְדָקָה מַצָּה

שַׁמָּשׁ טַלִּית בַּת יַיִן שַׁבָּת

Pictionary	English	Hebrew
	wine	_____ .1
	dreidel	_____ .2
	unleavened bread	_____ .3
	kippah	_____ .4
	helper candle	_____ .5
	prophet	_____ .6
	daughter	_____ .7
	Shabbat	_____ .8
	prayer shawl	_____ .9
	justice, *tzedakah*	_____ .10

New Letter
פ

Name _____

What's Missing?

Fill in the blank to complete the pattern in each row.

1. יַיִן _____ כַּפָּה יַיִן שׁוֹפָר כַּפָּה

2. טַלִית קָדוֹשׁ _____ טַלִית קָדוֹשׁ נֶפֶשׁ

3. _____ כֹּהֲנִים צִפּוֹרָה תְּפִלָה כֹּהֲנִים צִפּוֹרָה

4. צוֹפִיָה תּוֹרָה _____ צוֹפִיָה תּוֹרָה הַפְטָרָה

5. תִּפְתָּח _____ רֹאשׁ תִּפְתָּח אֲפִיקוֹמָן רֹאשׁ

Who Am I?

• I am the hidden treasure at the פֶּסַח seder.

   (Circle) my name in the words above.

• I am made from a ram's horn.

   Underline my name.

• You say Kiddush over me.

   Box my name.

• You wear me when you pray.

   Draw a squiggly line under my name.

   (Hint: There are two answers.)

Name _____

Bingo for One

Write the number of the Hebrew word in the matching English box.
Try to fill your entire bingo card.

13. בְּרָכָה	9. שְׁמַע	5. אֲרוֹן הַקֹּדֶשׁ	1. הַבְדָּלָה
14. אֱמֶת	10. צִיצִית	6. וְאָהַבְתָּ	2. מִנְיָן
15. חַלָּה	11. יוֹם טוֹב	7. שׁוֹפָר	3. תּוֹרָה
16. נֶפֶשׁ	12. עֲלִיָּה	8. יְצִיאַת מִצְרַיִם	4. צְדָקָה

Exodus from Egypt	knotted fringes	separation	ram's horn
Holy Ark	braided bread	justice	hear
soul	ten Jewish adults	blessing	teaching
holiday	and you shall love	truth	going up

Bingo Bonus

Fill in the missing English word.

_____ O Israel, Adonai is our God, Adonai is One.

Now write the missing word in Hebrew. _____

Name _____

Tic-Tac-Toe Travels

Play each tic-tac-toe game with a different reading partner. Read the word-parts and words correctly to make an X or an O.

①

אֹ	אִי	אֶ
אַ	אֱ	אִי
אְ	אוֹ	אָ

②

שָׁב	בֵּית	מֶן
טֶב	מִים	אֲכִי
לֹהֵי	שַׁח	סֶד

③

יִּים	פֵּר	סִים
נָּן	חֶס	נֵר
מֹעַ	דוֹשׁ	קוֹפֵ

④

תּוֹרָה	סֵפֶר	תָּמִיד
וַיֹּאמֶר	לֶחֶם	מַפְטִיר
מַלְאֲכִי	מֹשֶׁה	כָּמְכָה

Tic-Tac-Toe for Two

This tic-tac-toe game is missing its words. Choose nine words from the Heritage Word List at the back of your textbook and write one word neatly in each empty box. Then challenge a reading partner to play your game.

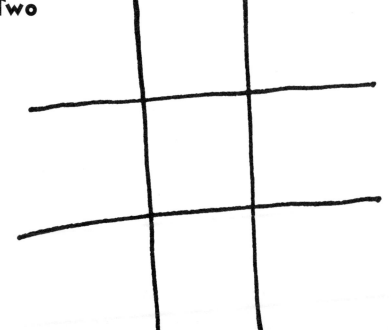

Name _____

Your Favorite Things

Fill in the missing word in each blessing ending.
Then read the blessing endings and answer the questions.

1. הָעֵץ

_____ בּוֹרֵי פְּרִי

Creator of the fruit of the tree

What is your favorite fruit? _____

2. הָאָרֶץ

_____ הַמּוֹצִיא לֶחֶם מִן

Who brings forth bread from the earth

What is your favorite sandwich? _____

3. הָאֲדָמָה

_____ בּוֹרֵא פְּרִי

Creator of the fruit of the earth

What is your favorite vegetable? _____

4. מַצָּה

_____ עַל אֲכִילַת

To eat matzah

What is your favorite spread to put on matzah? _____

5. נֵר

לְהַדְלִיק _____ שֶׁל שַׁבָּת

To light the Shabbat light(s)

Name another holiday on which we light candles. _____

Name _____

Sssssssh!

Put a dot on the *right* of each שׂ.

Then read the words.

1. שָׁלוֹם שֶׁמֶשׁ נֶפֶשׁ שָׁנָה שַׁבָּת שֶׁמֶשׁ

2. שֵׁבֶט שְׁלֹמֹה שִׁירָה יְשִׁיבָה נִשְׁתַּנָּה מִשְׁנָה

What sound does Shin make? _____

Put a dot on the *left* of each שׂ.

Then read the words.

3. שָׂם לַעֲשׂוֹת עוֹשֶׂה יִשְׂרָאֵל שָׂשׂוֹן שִׂים

4. עֶשֶׂר בַּשָּׂמִים לְשִׂמְחָה עֹשֶׂה עֲשֶׂרֶת שִׂמְחַת

What sound does Sin make? _____

Tongue Twisters

Can you read these שׂ - שׁ combinations without twisting your tongue?

1. שׂוֹשׁ שָׂשׁוֹ שָׂשׁ שֵׂשׁ שִׁישׂ שָׂשׁ שׁוֹשׂוֹ

2. שַׂשִׂי שֶׁשׁ שׂוֹשִׁי שִׁשִׁי שָׁשׁ שֶׂשׁ שֶׁשִׂי

3. שֶׁשׁ שׂוֹשִׁי שֶׁשׁ שֵׁשׁ שׂוֹשִׁי שֶׁשׁ שָׂשׁוֹ

Name _____

Visiting יִשְׂרָאֵל

Write the number of the Hebrew word next to its English meaning.

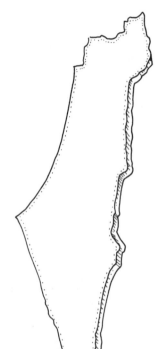

_____ The Hope   אֶרֶץ יִשְׂרָאֵל .1

_____ the (Western) Wall   הַכֹּתֶל .2

_____ Israeli Parliament   הַתִּקְוָה .3

_____ Land of Israel   עִבְרִית .4

_____ Hebrew   עֲלִיָה .5

_____ going up   צִיּוֹן .6

_____ State of Israel   מְדִינַת יִשְׂרָאֵל .7

_____ Zion   כְּנֶסֶת .8

Did You Know?

The word צִיּוֹן is the name of one of the hills in Jerusalem. The word צִיּוֹן is often used to represent the entire city of Jerusalem and even all of יִשְׂרָאֵל.

Write צִיּוֹן here. _____

From the Siddur

Read the prayer phrase below.

שְׁמַע יִשְׂרָאֵל

Circle the word that means Israel.

What does the other word mean? _____

Name _____

Making Faces

In each circle below draw a face (eyes, eyebrows, nose, mouth, ears, hair) to reflect
the emotion indicated by the Hebrew and English words.

   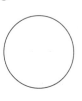

בַּיְשָׁן	עַקְשָׁן	פַּחְדָן	נִרְגָּשׁ	כּוֹעֵס	שָׂמֵחַ
bashful	stubborn	fearful	excited	angry	happy

I Have a Little Dreidel

Add the ending sound הּ to complete each word on the dreidels.
Read the words to a classmate.

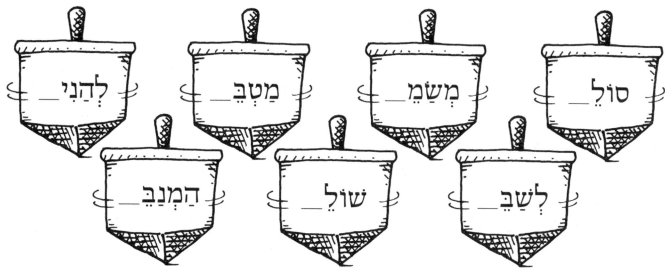

לְהָנִי ___   מַטְבֵּ ___   מִשְׁמַ ___   סוֹל ___

הַמְנַבֵּ ___   שׁוֹל ___   לְשַׁבֵּ ___

Spinning the Dreidel

Add the four letters found on the dreidel— נ, ג, ה, שׁ —in right-to-left order to

complete the phrase. ם ___ יָה ___ דוֹל ___ ס ___
Read the phrase.

What does it mean? _____

Name _____

A Jewish Star: מָגֵן דָּוִד

Write the correct heritage word inside each מָגֵן דָּוִד.

טַלִּית	יִשְׂרָאֵל	נֵר תָּמִיד	מְגִלָּה
חַג שָׂמֵחַ	צְדָקָה	מַלְכָּה	צִיצִית
עֵץ חַיִּים	הַגָּדָה	שַׁבָּת	סֵפֶר תּוֹרָה
שׁוֹפָר	שָׁלוֹם	מִצְווֹת	סֵדֶר

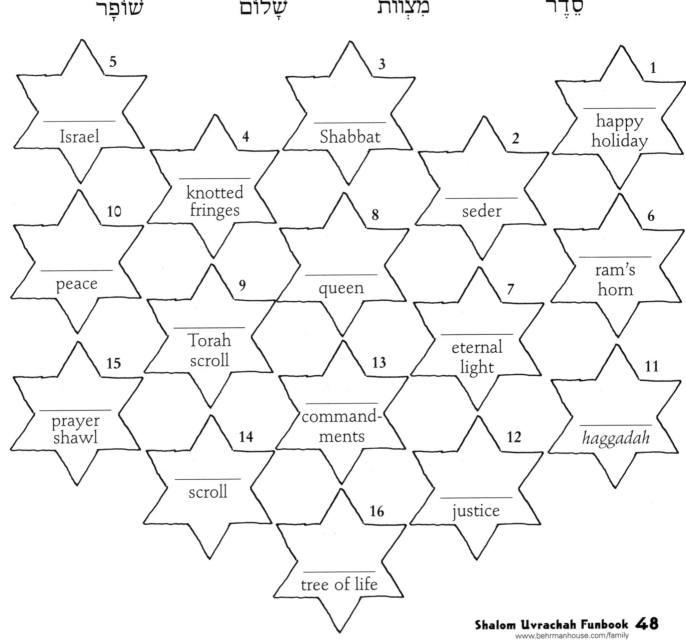

5 — Israel

4 — knotted fringes

3 — Shabbat

2 — seder

1 — happy holiday

10 — peace

9 — Torah scroll

8 — queen

7 — eternal light

6 — ram's horn

15 — prayer shawl

14 — scroll

13 — command-ments

12 — justice

11 — *haggadah*

16 — tree of life

Name _____

Dot It!

Add a dot to the **ו** in the word-parts below to make the vowel sound **וֹ**.

Read the word-parts to a classmate.

1. בּוֹ נוֹ מוֹ שׁוֹ תוֹ הוֹ קוֹ

2. לָנוּ בִּינוּ וָנוֹ הֵינוּ כֵּנוּ עֶנוּ יָנוּ

3. דוֹשׁ שָׁבוֹ פֶּצוּ דוֹר יָדוֹ רוֹשׁ הָיוּ

Add a dot to the **ו** in the words below to make the vowel sound **וֹ**.

Read the words to a classmate.

4. קָדוֹשׁ אֱלֹהֵינוּ יְרוּשָׁלַיִם פּוּרִים אֵלִיָּהוּ

Grapes into Wine

Write the vowel **וֹ** on all of the grapes in the bunch.

What sound does **וֹ** make? _____

Add **וֹ** to complete this word:

קָד__שׁ

When do we recite this blessing? _____

Read the blessing ending.

בּוֹרֵא פְּרִי הַגָּפֶן

Creator of the fruit of the vine

Name _____

The Five Books of Moses

The Torah is also known as the Five Books of Moses or the חֻמָשׁ.

Add the missing vowel to complete the word: חֻמָשׁ.

Below are the Hebrew names of the Five Books of Moses.
Write each Hebrew name on the matching book.

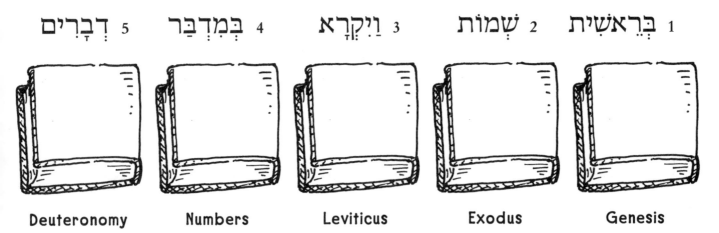

5 דְּבָרִים   4 בְּמִדְבַּר   3 וַיִּקְרָא   2 שְׁמוֹת   1 בְּרֵאשִׁית

Deuteronomy   Numbers   Leviticus   Exodus   Genesis

On Tour

Read the Hebrew city names.

Then write the number of the Hebrew city name next to the matching English.

5. חֵיפָה   4. אֵילַת   3. שִׁיקָגוֹ   2. יְרוּשָׁלַיִם   1. בּוֹסְטוֹן

10. צְפַת   9. נְיוּ-יוֹרְק   8. תֵּל-אָבִיב   7. דֶּנְבֶר   6. הוֹנְג קוֹנְג

Haifa ____   Eilat ____   Boston ____   Safed ____   Denver ____

Jerusalem ____   Chicago ____   New York ____   Tel Aviv ____   Hong Kong ____

Geography Know-Where

Which five cities are in יִשְׂרָאֵל?

Write their numbers. _____

Name _____

Moonbeams

Practice reading the names of the twelve Hebrew months.

Write the names in the moons.

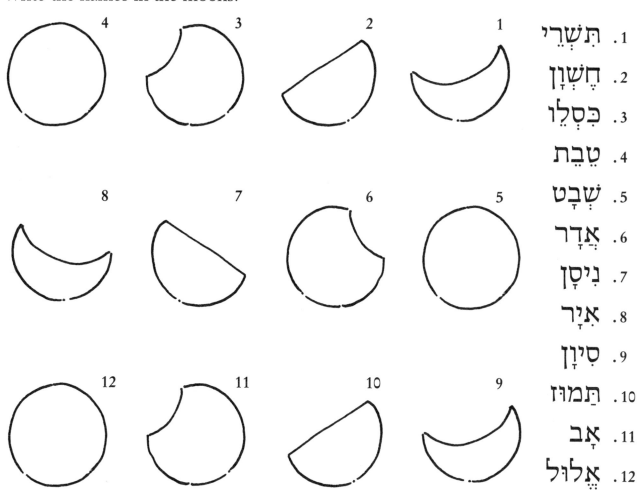

1. תִּשְׁרֵי
2. חֶשְׁוָן
3. כִּסְלֵו
4. טֵבֵת
5. שְׁבָט
6. אֲדָר
7. נִיסָן
8. אִיָּר
9. סִיוָן
10. תַּמּוּז
11. אָב
12. אֱלוּל

Did You Know?

The Jewish month begins when a new moon appears.

We call the first day of a new month רֹאשׁ חֹדֶשׁ — "head of the month."

Draw a new moon here.

New Letter
ז

Name _____

Hebrew Math

Hebrew letters stand for numbers.

$5 = $ ה $4 = $ ד $3 = $ ג $2 = $ ב $1 = $ א

$10 = $ י $9 = $ ט $8 = $ ח $7 = $ ז $6 = $ ו

Can you solve these math problems?

Have a classmate check your work.

____ = ה + ה .3	____ = ג − ז .2	____ = ב + א .1
____ = ז − ט .6	____ = ד + ו .5	____ = ח + י .4
____ = ד − י .9	____ = י + ג .8	____ = ו − ח .7
____ = ג + ה .12	____ = א + ט .11	____ = ז + ז .10

Your Turn!

Make up six of your own math problems using Hebrew letters.

Challenge a classmate to do the math!

____ = _____ .3	____ = _____ .2	____ = _____ .1
____ = _____ .6	____ = _____ .5	____ = _____ .4

To Life!

Add it up: ____ = י + ח

The Hebrew letters ח and י together form the word חַי — "life."

It is a Jewish tradition to make a צְדָקָה donation of $18 (or multiples of $18) to celebrate a happy occasion.

New Letter
ךְ

Name _____

Plant Your Roots

Hebrew words are built on roots.

The word בָּרוּךְ is built on the root ברכ, which means "bless" or "praise."

1 . Write one letter—ב,ר,כ—on each of the three roots of the tree—from right to left.

2 . Circle the three root letters in each Hebrew word growing on the tree.

Remember!

- The letters בּ and ב are members of the same letter family.

- The letters ךְ, כֹ, כ are members of the same letter family.

Think About It!

What does the root ברכ mean? _____

What would you praise God for in *your* life?

_____

Name _____

Blessing Dots

Say the words as you connect the "blessing dots."

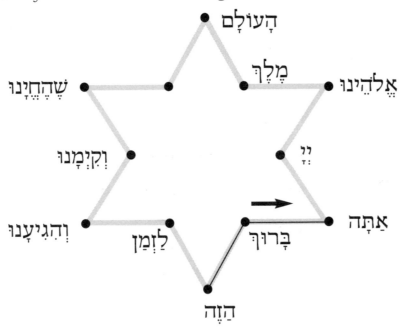

What shape did you draw? _____

Now read the entire blessing.

בָּרוּךְ אַתָּה יְיָ אֱלֹהֵינוּ מֶלֶךְ הָעוֹלָם
שֶׁהֶחֱיָנוּ וְקִיְּמָנוּ וְהִגִּיעָנוּ לַזְּמַן הַזֶּה.

בְּרָכָה A

We recite this בְּרָכָה when we celebrate something new or special in our lives, for example, a new home, a birthday, or the start of a Jewish holiday.

Is there something new or special in your life right now?

_____

L.O.L.

Read the sounds to laugh out loud in Hebrew.

ךְ ךְ ךְ ךְ ךְ

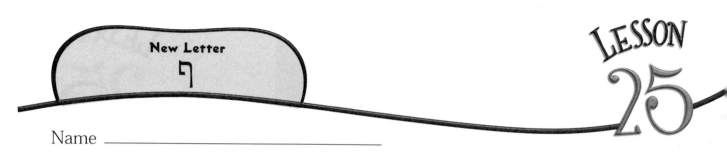

Name _____

Race Cars

Help the cars complete the race by writing the number of each letter name in the matching car.

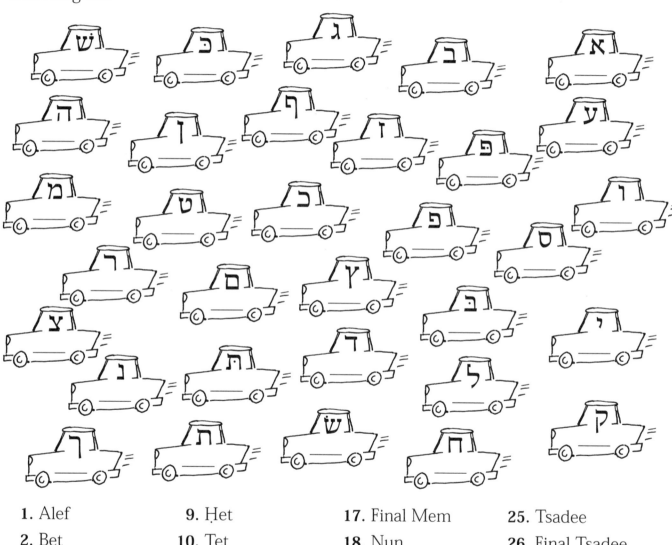

1. Alef	**9.** Het	**17.** Final Mem	**25.** Tsadee
2. Bet	**10.** Tet	**18.** Nun	**26.** Final Tsadee
3. Vet	**11.** Yud	**19.** Final Nun	**27.** Koof
4. Gimmel	**12.** Kaf	**20.** Samech	**28.** Resh
5. Dalet	**13.** Chaf	**21.** Ayin	**29.** Shin
6. Hay	**14.** Final Chaf	**22.** Pay	**30.** Sin
7. Vav	**15.** Lamed	**23.** Fay	**31.** Tav
8. Zayin	**16.** Mem	**24.** Final Fay	**32.** Tav

New Letter

ף

Name _____

Word Find

Below are 12 heritage words. Find and circle the English meaning of each word in the puzzle. The English words appear from left to right or from top to bottom.

(Hint: Sometimes letters found in one word are part of another word.)

9. קָדוֹשׁ   5. כַּלָה   1. שַׁבָּת

10. שְׁמַע   6. מִצְוָה   2. צְדָקָה

11. אֱמֶת   7. תּוֹרָה   3. עֲלִיָה

12. יִשְׂרָאֵל   8. מְזוּזָה   4. שׁוֹפָר

G	C	B	R	I	D	E	X	L	K
O	O	J	S	H	O	F	A	R	I
I	M	U	Y	R	K	V	D	L	D
N	M	S	H	A	B	B	A	T	D
G	A	T	J	E	R	T	N	O	U
U	N	I	A	L	H	R	I	R	S
P	D	C	M	E	Z	U	Z	A	H
W	M	E	P	S	Z	T	J	H	U
X	E	U	G	L	I	H	E	A	R
H	N	A	R	K	E	F	O	M	Z
E	T	R	I	S	R	A	E	L	O

What's My Line?

Use each of the heritage words in an English sentence.

For example: "We recite קָדוֹשׁ on Friday night."

You can write the sentences on the back of this page or on another sheet of paper or you can tell them to a friend.